Mark Time

Standard and Advanced Study Courses

Suitable for Correspondence and Group Studies

A straightforward way of studying Mark's Gospel

with an easy-to-use set of questions

based on Mark Time (the Book) by Gerard Chrispin

PART 2

DayOne

First Printed 2011

Second edition © 2012–with corrections, modifications and amendments to the First edition

This edition © 2019

ISBN 978-1-84625-661-5

Published by Day One Publications
Ryelands Road, Leominster, HR6 8NZ
Tel 01568 613 740
email–sales@dayone.co.uk
website–www.dayone.co.uk

Mark Time–the Study Course

Please fill in your details below:

Name: Rhea Bonela

ID No.:

Establishment:

Location: Crangord baptist church

Marker's Comments

Contents

Mark Time–the Study Course

on Mark's Gospel

with an easy-to-use set of questions based on Mark Time–the Book

Getting to grips with Mark Time–the Study Course

Answering the Questions and Planning your Study Time

Welcome to Mark Time–the Study Course — PART 2! May God bless you and make you a blessing to others as you use it.

Straightforward Steps to follow:

Answering the Standard Questions*—PRAY BEFORE ANSWERING ANY OF THE QUESTIONS AND ASK THE LORD TO HELP YOU.*

1. *Read Chapter 28 of Mark Time–the Book*
2. *Read the Scriptures given in Paper 28 in this study book*
3. *Answer each question (where there is a tick box) by ticking the correct answer.*
4. *For sentence answers write clearly and if possible in black.*
5. *Repeat for the remaining 24 papers.*

Answering the Advanced Questions*—this is optional, but why not give it a try!*

1. *Choose one question from the three given*
2. *Fill in the answer box—do not write more*
3. *Leave the Marker's comments box empty*

A Study Plan

1. *Decide how many Papers you will complete each day.*
   If you do 4 Papers per day you will complete in 1 week
   If you do 2 Papers per day you will complete in 2 weeks
2. *Complete all 25 Papers before submitting your Papers for marking.*

Application

Always look through your answers and find things to do in your own life as you trust the Lord to help you.

Submitting the Answers

Page 3 of the study booklet must be filled out with your details. ID numbers are for the armed forces or residents within establishments.

The last page is where you send them. Churches or Christian organisations may affix a sticker with returning information here.

If you are studying within an HMPPS or an Immigration Removal Centre submit your answers to your chaplain.

If you are studying with a church or another Christian organisation ask them how they would like you to submit your answers unless it is already given through the sticker on the rear page.

1 21/4

Paper 28

Bread and blindness Mark 8:1-26

Q1 **Compare Jesus' feeding of the large crowd in Mark 6:33–44 with the large crowd in Mark 8:1–9.**

Please answer (a) from the account in Mark 6:33–44 and (b) from the account in Mark 8:1–9

State how many	Men	(a)	(b)
	Loaves	(a)	(b)
	Fish	(a)	(b)
	Baskets	(a)	(b)

Q2 **How does Mark 18:19–20 help you to be clear about what happened?**

- ☐ It denies there are two miracles
- ☐ It is unclear itself
- ☐ It clearly records Jesus confirming both miracles

Q3 **At Dalmanutha what do the Pharisees ask for from Jesus that causes Him to sigh in His spirit? (vv.11–12)**

- ☐ To teach God's word
- ☐ To go away
- ☐ To produce a sign from heaven (even after His recent miracles!)

Q4 **Before leaving for the other side of Galilee, how does Jesus respond to their request for a sign? (vv.12–13)**

- ☐ He asks 'Why?' and says 'No!'
- ☐ He promises them a huge miracle
- ☐ He ignores them

Q5 **What have the disciples forgotten to bring? (vv.14, 16)**

- ☐ Fishing nets
- ☐ Ropes
- ☐ Bread, except for one loaf

Q6 **What is the first discussion point arising from the disciples having forgotten the bread? (v.15)**

- ☐ Beware of the pride of the Pharisees and Herod ('leaven' or yeast)
- ☐ Being hungry
- ☐ Forgetfulness

Q7 **Why does Jesus question the hardness of the disciples' hearts and their poor understanding? (vv.17–21)**

- ☐ Because they grumble
- ☐ Because they forget His two 'feeding' miracles
- ☐ Because they don't pray

Q8 **Answer briefly in what ways the healing of this blind man is similar to other miracles performed by Jesus. In what way is it different? Does it teach you anything? (vv.22–26)**

____

____

____

____

____

Marker's comments: do not write in this box

Paper 28 – Advanced Study

Students for the Advanced Study should answer one of A, B or C below

A. **How do you know that this further account of feeding thousands of people with hardly any food is not a confused contradiction of the first account?**
Mark 8:6–9; Mark 6:41; Mark 8:19–20; 2 Timothy 2:15

B. **Compare the blindness of the Pharisees with the blindness of the disciples.** Mark 8:14–21; Mark 8:11–12, 15; Matthew 15:12–14; Revelation 3:18; 1 John 2:8–11

C. **In what ways is the healing of this blind man similar to other miracles performed by Jesus? In what way is it different?**
Mark 8:22–25

PLEASE keep answers within the boxes provided

My answer (in between 150 and 300 words)

My answer continued

Marker's comments: do not write in this box

Paper 29

Questions Jesus asks — Mark 8:27-38

Q1 **What is the disciples' answer in Caesarea Philippi when Jesus asks who people say He is? (vv.27–28)**

- ☐ Abraham, Isaac or Jacob
- ☐ David, Solomon or Hezekiah
- ☐ John the Baptist, Elijah or a prophet

Q2 **When Peter answers that he believes Jesus is the Christ, what warning does Jesus give him? (vv.29–30)**

- ☐ Do not keep quiet about it
- ☐ Tell no-one about it
- ☐ Don't keep guessing like that

Q3 **What does Jesus begin to teach very plainly about how he, the Son of Man, will suffer? (vv.31–32)**

- ☐ By poverty
- ☐ By criticism
- ☐ In many ways, by rejection, and by death—then rise again after three days

Q4 **Who influences Peter to rebuke Jesus for predicting His suffering, death and resurrection? (vv.32–33)**

- ☐ Peter himself
- ☐ Satan
- ☐ The other disciples

Q5 **What does Jesus teach that it will take to take to follow Him as a disciple? (vv.34–35)**

- ☐ Self denial and dying to self-will
- ☐ Joining a church
- ☐ Fasting for Lent

Q6 **If to gain the whole world you had to lose your own eternal soul, would that be a good deal? (vv.35–37)**

- ☐ Yes
- ☐ No
- ☐ Not sure

Q7 **What will people find out too late who have been too ashamed of Jesus to trust and follow Him? (v.38)**

- ☐ Jesus will be ashamed of them at the second coming
- ☐ Nothing bad
- ☐ i don't know or care

Marker's comments: do not write in this box

Paper 29 – Advanced Study

Students for the Advanced Study should answer one of A, B or C below

A. **What does Peter get right here? Why is that important?**
Mark 8:29; John 14:6; Acts 4:12; Matthew 1:21

B. **What does Peter get sadly wrong? Why is it important to get the issue of Jesus' death right?**
Mark 8:31–33; Hebrews 9:22; Luke 19:10; 1 Corinthians 15:3–4

C. **What does Jesus teach is the value of an eternal soul? Why does knowing that your soul is safe for eternity encourage you to deny yourself in order to follow Jesus?**
Mark 8:34–38; Luke 14:27

PLEASE keep answers within the boxes provided

My answer (in between 150 and 300 words)

My answer continued

Marker's comments: do not write in this box

Paper 30

Jesus only

Mark 9:1-13

Q1 Before taking Peter, James and John up a mountain, what does Jesus say some disciples will see? (v.1)

- ☐ His ascension to heaven
- ☐ His second coming
- ☐ The kingdom of God after it has come with power

Q2 As Jesus' clothes become amazingly and radiantly white, who appears talking with Him? (vv.3–4)

- ☐ Stephen and Andrew
- ☐ Moses and Elijah
- ☐ Abraham and Noah

Q3 What does terrified Peter ignorantly suggest that they make for Moses, Elijah and Jesus? (vv.5–6)

- ☐ A tent each
- ☐ Breakfast
- ☐ A monument

Q4 To whom does the voice from the cloud say they must listen? Whom do they see after that? (vv. 7, 8)

- ☐ No-one; Moses
- ☐ God's beloved Son; Jesus only
- ☐ Elijah; An angel

Q5 **Why will they not tell everyone else what they have seen until after Jesus is resurrected? (vv.9–10)**

- ☐ They are too embarrassed
- ☐ They are too scared
- ☐ Jesus tells them not to share it until then

Q6 **What do they not understand? (v.10)**

- ☐ The rising from the dead
- ☐ Where Moses has gone
- ☐ Why Elijah was selected to be there

Q7 **Jesus says what about**

(a) someone fulfilling Elijah's role (John the Baptist?) (vv.11–13)

- ☐ Elijah won't come
- ☐ Elijah has come, as he had to, and has suffered from others
- ☐ He is Elijah

(b) Himself? (vv.11–13)

- ☐ Jesus will be well treated
- ☐ Jesus will suffer many things and contempt
- ☐ Jesus will disappear

Marker's comments: do not write in this box

Paper 30 – Advanced Study

Students for the Advanced Study should answer one of A, B or C below

A. **How does the transfiguration of Jesus on the mountain fulfil the prediction that some will not taste death until they see the kingdom of God coming with power?** Mark 9:1–3

B. **What do you learn from the fact that only Jesus remains after Elijah and Moses depart? What do Elijah and Moses represent?** Hebrews 1:1–2; 2 Chronicles 21:12 (first half); Malachi 4:5; John 1:17; Hebrews 3:1–6; John 7:19; Acts 13:39; Romans 10:5

C. **What good example do the disciples give when they are confused about understanding what Jesus has said?** Mark 9:11; Acts 17:11; Matthew 7:7–8; James 1:5

PLEASE keep answers within the boxes provided

My answer (in between 150 and 300 words)

My answer continued

Marker's comments: do not write in this box

Paper 31

The prayer God always answers — Mark 9:14-29

Q1 **What was the crowd at the foot of the mountain arguing about with Jesus' other disciples? (vv.14–18)**

- ☐ Why Jesus' disciples could not expel a mute spirit from a boy
- ☐ Where Jesus was
- ☐ Religious freedom

Q2 **In asking them to bring the boy to Him, what does Jesus say His disciples lack? (v.19)**

- ☐ Power
- ☐ Honesty
- ☐ Faith

Q3 **Why now does the spirit convulse the boy, making him roll on the ground and foam at the mouth? (v.20)**

- ☐ It sees Jesus
- ☐ It reacts to crowds
- ☐ No special reason

Q4 **Since childhood what two dangers does the child face through the mute spirit's convulsions? (vv.21–22)**

- ☐ Animals and reptiles
- ☐ Fire and water
- ☐ Getting lost and losing memory

Q5 **After discussing if Jesus can help and the need for faith, what does the father pray to Jesus? (vv.22–24)**

- ☐ 'I believe; help my unbelief'
- ☐ 'Expel the mute spirit'
- ☐ 'Save my son'

Q6 **What event triggers Jesus' rebuking and expelling forever the mute spirit from the boy? (vv.25–26)**

- ☐ The father breaks down
- ☐ The convulsion gets worse
- ☐ Jesus sees a crowd running towards them

Q7 **After cries, convulsions and expelling the spirit, how does Jesus raise the seemingly dead boy? (vv.26–27)**

- ☐ He takes his hand and lifts him up
- ☐ He anoints him with oil
- ☐ He asks everyone to lay hands on him

Q8 **What does Jesus tell the disciples is needed to drive out this kind of mute spirit? (vv.28–29)**

- ☐ Singing lots of emotional hymns and choruses
- ☐ Supernatural healing powers
- ☐ Prayer

Marker's comments: do not write in this box

Paper 31 – Advanced Study

Students for the Advanced Study should answer one of A, B or C below

A. **After a time of blessing on the mountain what do the disciples encounter with Jesus? Should you expect Satan to attack after a time of blessing?** Mark 9:14–18; Matthew 3:16–17; Matthew 4:1–11; 2 Corinthians 12:7; Job 1:6–12

B. **Although the way that Jesus heals the spirit-possessed mute boy is another historical fact, how does it also illustrate how God works in a sinner who turns to Christ as his Saviour?** Matthew 11:28; Ephesians 2:1; Romans 8:2

C. **If you are assaulted by unbelief and doubts, how should you deal with them? How should your prayers be affected?** Mark 9:24; Romans 10:17; Acts 17:31

PLEASE keep answers within the boxes provided

My answer (in between 150 and 300 words)

My answer continued

Marker's comments: do not write in this box

Paper 32

Important teaching on important subjects

Mark 9:30-50

Q1 **What does Jesus teach the disciples privately that they do not grasp and fear to ask Him about? (vv.30–32)**

- ☐ His coming death and resurrection
- ☐ The best route through Galilee
- ☐ How to be successful

Q2 **After arguments about greatness, by whom does Jesus reveal real humble leadership quality? (vv.33–37)**

- ☐ A famous king
- ☐ A wealthy businessman
- ☐ A child

Q3 **How does Jesus want His disciples to view other people who serve Him and His cause? (vv.38–40)**

- ☐ As competitors to beat by their results
- ☐ Gratefully, as working for the same Lord
- ☐ As enemies to oppose

Q4 **What will Jesus do for those who show even a small kindness and help to fellow Christians? (v.41)**

- ☐ He will punish them
- ☐ He will ignore them
- ☐ He will reward them

Q5 **How does Jesus say those who offend little ones who believe in Him should be treated? (v.42)**

- ☐ Very harshly
- ☐ Softly
- ☐ Indifferently

Q6 **Given Jesus' teaching on hell's unquenchable fire, how should we deal with ourselves? (vv.42–49)**

- ☐ Be gentle to ourselves
- ☐ Take strongest action to avoid sin and to repent
- ☐ Avoid thinking about it

Q7 **If we maintain our Christian 'saltiness' how will our dealings with each other be characterised? (v.50)**

- ☐ Coldness
- ☐ Conflict
- ☐ Peace

Marker's comments: do not write in this box

Paper 32 – Advanced Study

Students for the Advanced Study should answer one of A, B or C below

A. **Why does Jesus often remind the disciples that He must suffer, die and rise again? Why are His death and resurrection so very important?** Mark 9:30–32; Acts 26:22–23; Luke 24:45–47; John 11:49–53; Acts 4:12

B. **Why are the disciples shamed into silence at Jesus' question? What personal ambition should a Christian have?**
Mark 9:33–35; Philippians 2:3–11; Matthew 6:33; Matthew 16:24

C. **Consider God's hatred for sin. How will He judge those who sinfully cause His children to suffer? What do the severe illustrations of avoiding sinning teach about how to follow Christ?**
Mark 9:42–47; Romans 1:18; Romans 12:1–2; Luke 9:23

PLEASE keep answers within the boxes provided

My answer (in between 150 and 300 words)

My answer continued

Marker's comments: do not write in this box

Paper 33

How about divorce? Mark 10:1-12

Q1 **As Jesus teaches in Judea beyond the Jordan who tests Him with a question about divorce? (vv.1–2)**

- ☐ A Samaritan
- ☐ Pharisees
- ☐ A Priest

Q2 **Asked if it is lawful for a man to divorce his wife, to whom and to what does Jesus refer him? (vv.2–3)**

- ☐ Moses and the Scriptures
- ☐ The Sanhedrin and man's traditions
- ☐ The Governor and Roman law

Q3 **Why did Moses allow (but not command) divorce by a certificate of divorce? (vv.4–5)**

- ☐ To please the Romans
- ☐ Because he hated women
- ☐ Because of their hard hearts

Q4 **What two parties are a party to marriage since creation, according to Jesus? (v.6)**

- ☐ Rich and poor
- ☐ Male and female
- ☐ Black and white

Q5 **To show that a man and wife are no longer two, but one flesh, what two things must the man do? (vv.7–8)**

☐ Work and protect his wife

☐ Build a house and hunt animals

☐ Leave his parents and hold fast to his wife

Q6 **Who does Jesus say puts marriages together and therefore man must not separate them? (v.9)**

☐ God

☐ The church

☐ The synagogue

Q7 **When the disciples later question Him, how does Jesus describe adultery? (vv.10–12)**

☐ Divorcing a spouse and marrying another

☐ Getting fed up and and leaving

☐ Having immoral habits

Q8 **How does Matthew 5:31–32 explain legitimate divorce, thus allowing remarriage without adultery?**

☐ If both parties agree

☐ If the ground is sexual immorality

☐ If one party now hates the other

Marker's comments: do not write in this box

Paper 33 – Advanced Study

Students for the Advanced Study should answer one of A, B or C below

A. **What is God's best plan for marriage? Does the Bible anywhere teach that it is right for a man and a woman to live together and have sexual relationships outside marriage?**
Mark 10:6–9; 1 Corinthians 6:18; Exodus 20:14;
Mark 10:19; Colossians 3:5; Ephesians 5:3; Galatians 5:19;
2 Corinthians 12:21

B. **What is Jesus' blended teaching in Mark 10:11–12 and Matthew 5:31–32 on this ground for divorce? Consider this in the light of 1 Peter 3:7, Ephesians 5:25, and Colossians 3:19. What other possible biblical ground for divorce is later given through the apostle Paul in 1 Corinthians 7:10–16 especially verse 15?**
Mark 10:11–12; Matthew 5:31–32; 1 Peter 3:7; Ephesians 5:25;
Colossians 3:19

C. **Why should a Christian strive to save his or her marriage, if at all possible?** Mark 10:6–9; 1 Peter 3:1–7

PLEASE keep answers within the boxes provided

My answer (in between 150 and 300 words)

My answer continued

Marker's comments: do not write in this box

Paper 34

A clear contrast—children and the rich young man
Mark 10:13-31

Q1 Contrast Jesus' attitude with His disciples' attitude about letting little children to come to Him. (vv.13–16)

- ☐ He welcomes and blesses them, they rebuke them
- ☐ He and they rebuke them
- ☐ He and they welcome them

Q2 What does Jesus say we must receive like a child in order to enter it? (vv.14–16)

- ☐ Religious truth
- ☐ The kingdom of God
- ☐ Freedom from sin

Q3 Calling Jesus 'Good Teacher' what is the man wanting to have? (v.17)

- ☐ More wealth
- ☐ Eternal life
- ☐ Popularity

Q4 If God alone is perfectly good and if Jesus is perfectly good, then who is Jesus? (vv.17–18)

- ☐ Just a good man
- ☐ God as well as man
- ☐ God but not man

Q5 **Which of the last six commandments in Exodus 20:12–17 does Jesus *not* quote to the man? (vv.17–20)**

- ☐ He misses none but quotes them all
- ☐ 'You must go to church'
- ☐ 'You shall not covet'

Q6 **The man wrongly says he has broken no commandment. What makes him feel sad now: why? (vv.20–22)**

- ☐ Jesus says to sell his things and give cash to the poor: he is rich
- ☐ Honesty: he cheats
- ☐ Nothing: he is glad

Q7 **It seems impossible for the rich to enter God's kingdom. Why and how can any be saved? (vv.23–27)**

- ☐ God may decide to save everyone
- ☐ By living a good life
- ☐ Because nothing is impossible for God

Q8 **What will accompany the benefits which Christ's followers will receive as well as eternal life? (vv.28–31)**

- ☐ Praise from men
- ☐ Rewards from governments
- ☐ Persecution

Marker's comments: do not write in this box

Paper 34 – Advanced Study

Students for the Advanced Study should answer one of A, B or C below

A. **How is childlikeness a good example of how to put your trust in Jesus Christ?** Mark 10:14–15; Matthew 18:1–4

B. **How does Jesus get to the real heart of the problem of the poor rich man?**
Mark 10:21–25; Exodus 20:17; Luke 12:15–21

C. **Did the man claim more about his righteousness and relationship with God than he actually experienced in practice? How can we deal with that temptation?**
Mark 10:20; Psalm 51:6; Matthew 6:33; Colossians 3:2

PLEASE keep answers within the boxes provided

My answer (in between 150 and 300 words)

My answer continued

Marker's comments: do not write in this box

Paper 35

Reminded, rebuked and restored — Mark 10:32-52

Q1 **Why does Jesus remind the disciples again of His coming suffering, death and resurrection? (vv.32–34)**

- ☐ They have already forgotten
- ☐ When He dies and rises again He wants them to remember
- ☐ No reason

Q2 **What do James and John, Zebedee's sons, want most? (vv.35–37)**

- ☐ The highest place of power in glory
- ☐ Peace and protection
- ☐ To serve Christ better

Q3 **Probably meaning suffering, what does Jesus say that they will drink and be baptised with? (vv.38–39)**

- ☐ Wine and water
- ☐ His cup (of suffering?) and His baptism (of suffering?)
- ☐ Holy water and holy water

Q4 **Jesus says He cannot give them seats of honour. What does He say about those places? (v.40)**

- ☐ There are none
- ☐ They are for the religious chiefs
- ☐ They have already been prepared for others

Q5 **Answering the ten's anger at James and John, what does Jesus say is the mark of true greatness? (vv.41–44)**

☐ Willing servant-hood or slavery

☐ A 'big' personality and great gifts

☐ Toughness in leading others

Q6 **What does Jesus call Himself when He says He came to serve and to die as a ransom for many? (v.45)**

☐ Emmanuel

☐ Almighty God

☐ The Son of Man

Q7 **What first two prayers of Bartimaeus does Jesus answer despite his being told to be silent? (vv.46–52)**

☐ 'Give me my sight'

☐ 'Have mercy on me'

☐ 'Work a miracle, please'

Q8 **To what does Jesus attribute the answer to verse 52's prayer as he responds to Christ's call? (vv.49–52)**

☐ Bartimaeus' pushing himself forward

☐ The encouragement of verse 49

☐ Bartimaeus' faith

Marker's comments: do not write in this box

Paper 35 – Advanced Study

Students for the Advanced Study should answer one of A, B or C below

A. **Here again, Jesus reminds His disciples about His coming rejection, suffering and death? Why do you think He reminds them of this so soon after the last warning?** Mark 10:32–34; 1 Timothy 4:6; 1 Corinthians 11:24–25; Exodus 20:8; John 16:4

B. **What are the two main reasons stated why Jesus came? How does His example compare with some rulers?** Mark 10:42–45

C. **Consider how Jesus deals with blind Bartimaeus. What lessons do you learn about helping those who 'cannot see' the truth of the gospel?** Mark 10:46–52

PLEASE keep answers within the boxes provided

My answer (in between 150 and 300 words)

My answer continued

Marker's comments: do not write in this box

Paper 36

Jesus at Jerusalem — Mark 11:1-11

Q1 Where do Jesus and His disciples now approach? (v.1)

- ☐ Capernaum
- ☐ Jericho
- ☐ Jerusalem, Bethphage and Bethany

Q2 Can you tell that Jesus is control from the way that two of His disciples collect the colt? Why? (vv.2–6)

- ☐ Yes. It happened just as He said
- ☐ No—just a coincidence
- ☐ No. Some was planned and some just luck

Q3 What does Jesus do when some cloaks are thrown on the unbroken colt? (v.7)

- ☐ Walks beside it
- ☐ Ignores it and rides in a carriage
- ☐ Sits on it

Q4 What is spread in the road before Jesus on the colt? Why do you think that is? (v.8)

- ☐ Hay and straw to feed colt
- ☐ Cloaks and leafy branches to show submission
- ☐ Grass to make road soft

Q5 What does 'Hosanna!' mean? (vv.9–10)

- ☐ Praise God!
- ☐ Bravo!
- ☐ Save now!

Q6 **What do the shouting crowd get right in verse 9?**

- ☐ Jesus is 'Blessed' and comes 'in the name of the Lord'
- ☐ Nothing
- ☐ He is a military leader

Q7 **What else do they get right in verse 10, remembering that Messiah is in the line of King David?**

- ☐ Jesus' biological parent is King David
- ☐ Jesus is Messiah in David's line
- ☐ Nothing—it is all wrong

Q8 **In Jerusalem, before returning to Bethany, what does Jesus take time to look around? (v.11)**

- ☐ A theatre
- ☐ Gethsemane
- ☐ The temple

Marker's comments: do not write in this box

Paper 36 – Advanced Study

Students for the Advanced Study should answer one of A, B or C below

A. **What do you notice about the sovereignty of our Lord Jesus Christ? What shows He is in control?**
Mark 11:1–6

B. **'Hosanna' means 'save now'? What do you think the crowd means by that? Why did they later cry 'Crucify Him'?**
Mark 11:9–10; Mark 15:13–14; 1 Peter 3:18

C. **What does Jesus do when He goes to the temple? How important is it to be properly informed before you act on an important issue?** Mark 11:11; Mark 11:15–19

PLEASE keep answers within the boxes provided

My answer (in between 150 and 300 words)

My answer continued

Marker's comments: do not write in this box

Paper 37

Straight talk

Mark 11:12-33

Q1 Between Bethany and Jerusalem what does Jesus, who is hungry, do to the barren fig tree? (vv.12–14)

- ☐ He curses it (without bad language), forbidding it to bear fruit
- ☐ He cuts it down
- ☐ He ignores it

Q2 Why does Jesus drive out of the temple buyers, sellers, money changers and market porters? (vv.15–17)

- ☐ Misuse of God's house of prayer for robbery
- ☐ He does not like the stench
- ☐ Their prices are too high

Q3 Why do the chief priests and scribes want to destroy Jesus? (v.18)

- ☐ They hate His miracles
- ☐ He knows so much
- ☐ Fear of Him because His teaching astonishes the crowd

Q4 Having left Jerusalem in the evening, on the next morning what do the disciples notice? (vv.19–21)

- ☐ It is raining
- ☐ The cursed fig tree has already withered to its roots
- ☐ The fig tree now bears fruit

Q5 **When Peter draws it to Jesus' attention, what does He tell them? (vv.21–22)**

- ☐ To ignore it
- ☐ Not to eat figs
- ☐ To have faith in God

Q6 **Using moving a mountain as a picture of answered prayer, what should go if we believe God? (vv.23–24)**

- ☐ Grumbling
- ☐ Doubts
- ☐ Persevering in prayer

Q7 **When we are praying what should we do towards people who have offended us in some way? (v.25)**

- ☐ Grumble at them
- ☐ Stop praying to write them a nasty letter
- ☐ Forgive them

Q8 **When the religious people try to trap Jesus with a question, how does Jesus answer? (vv.27–33)**

- ☐ He shouts at them
- ☐ He won't answer
- ☐ Carefully, thoughtfully, and by asking them a return question

Marker's comments: do not write in this box

Paper 37 – Advanced Study

Students for the Advanced Study should answer one of A, B or C below

A. **From this passage what lessons can you learn from the fig tree and about Jesus?** Mark 11:12–14; Mark 11:19–26

B. **Why is Jesus so strongly opposed to the misuse and abuse of the temple? As the Christian's body is referred to as 'the temple of the Holy Spirit' in 1 Corinthians 6:19, how does the way Jesus regards the temple challenge Christians today?**
Mark 11:15–17; 1 Corinthians 6:19–20; Romans 12:1–2

C. **What can you learn from Jesus about how to answer a tricky question intended to trap you?**
Mark 11:27–33; Mark 12:13–17

PLEASE keep answers within the boxes provided

My answer (in between 150 and 300 words)

My answer continued

Marker's comments: do not write in this box

Paper 38

Setting traps for Jesus — Mark 12:1-27

Q1 As questions to trap Jesus increase, what does He now use to teach His hearers? (v.1)

- ☐ Jokes
- ☐ Fairy stories based on imagination
- ☐ Parables based on fact

Q2 Note three similarities between Jesus' vineyard parable and the events leading to His death. (vv.2–11)

____

____

____

____

____

Q3 As Jesus' scared enemies go, knowing He criticises them, who put a tax-trap question to Him? (vv.12–14)

- ☐ Priests and Levites
- ☐ Romans and Greeks
- ☐ Pharisees and Herodians

Q4 To avoid publicly criticising Israel's Roman occupiers, what does Jesus ask about their coins? (vv.14–16)

- ☐ Whose features and name are on the coin?
- ☐ How heavy is it?
- ☐ How old is it?

Q5 **When told 'Caesar's', how does Jesus answer their cynical trick tax question, so that they marvel? (v.17)**

- ☐ Give all to Caesar
- ☐ Give all to God
- ☐ Give Caesar what is due to Caesar and God what is due to God

Q6 **What do the Sadducees refuse to believe in that makes them try to trick Jesus with a question? (v.18)**

- ☐ That God exists
- ☐ The resurrection
- ☐ The ten commandments

Q7 **What is wrong in their basic thinking leading to the story about a woman and seven husbands? (vv.19–27)**

- ☐ They don't know the Scriptures or God's power
- ☐ They accept Greek myths
- ☐ They are too clever

Q8 **What specific errors are there in that fanciful story leading to the trick question to trap Jesus? (vv.25–27)**

- ☐ The story could not happen
- ☐ No errors
- ☐ No marriage exists in heaven: God is the God of the living

Marker's comments: do not write in this box

Paper 38 – Advanced Study

Students for the Advanced Study should answer one of A, B or C below

A. **How does the parable about the vineyard mirror the religious leaders' opposition to Jesus?**
Mark 12:1–8; Mark 10:32–34; Matthew 23:28–32; Mark 15:15–28

B. **Consider the questions in verses 13 and 14 put to trick Jesus. Why does His answer amaze them?**
Mark 12:13–17; Romans 13:1–7

C. **What important truth do the Sadducees attack? What are their two big errors? To prove the resurrection how does Jesus blend Bible and logic?**
Mark 12:18–27; Romans 8:34; 2 Timothy 2:15; 2 Timothy 3:16

PLEASE keep answers within the boxes provided

My answer (in between 150 and 300 words)

My answer continued

Marker's comments: do not write in this box

Paper 39

Sincerity, deity, hypocrisy and generosity

Mark 12:28-44

Q1 **From verses 28 to 34 what shows that the scribe questioning Jesus is sincere and near God's kingdom?**

- ☐ He is not!
- ☐ He looks nice
- ☐ His is courteous, listens and comments wisely: and Jesus says he is near

Q2 **What does Jesus say summarises all the ten commandments (found in Exodus 20:1–17)? (vv.29–31)**

- ☐ Love and forgive yourself
- ☐ Be kind whenever possible
- ☐ Love God totally and love others as yourself

Q3 **If David, an ancestor of Jesus', called Him 'Lord' who is Jesus as well as being human? (vv.35–37)**

- ☐ A magician
- ☐ God
- ☐ An angel

Q4 **Of whom does Jesus tell the people to beware? (vv.38–40)**

- ☐ Kings
- ☐ Scribes
- ☐ Criminals

Q5 **Why must the people beware of the scribes? (vv.38–40)**

- ☐ They are violent
- ☐ They are immoral
- ☐ They are self-seeking hypocrites trying to impress

Q6 **Thinking about impressing others, who seem at first most impressive in terms of big gifts? (vv.41–44)**

- ☐ The rich people giving large sums
- ☐ The showy scribes
- ☐ The poor widow giving only two copper coins

Q7 **Who does Jesus say actually gave the most, and why? (vv.43–44)**

- ☐ The big donors–they gave big sums
- ☐ The poor widow—she gave her all

Q8 **Review the scribes, the rich people, and the poor widow: what is most important to God? (vv.38–44)**

- ☐ Wealth and show
- ☐ Inward devotion
- ☐ Looking respectable on the outside

Marker's comments: do not write in this box

Paper 39 – Advanced Study

Students for the Advanced Study should answer one of A, B or C below

A. **How do the two commandments, regarded as the greatest by Jesus, summarise the Ten Commandments so well?**
Exodus 20:1–17; Mark 12:29–34; Romans 14:9

B. **What does Jesus' logic in verses 35–37 teach you about who He really is?** Mark 12:35–37; 2 Peter 1:21; John 10:35–37

C. **Why does Jesus regard the poor widow as the most generous person in the temple, and what challenging lesson does it put to Christians about giving to God's work?**
Mark 12:41–44; 2 Corinthians 8:12

PLEASE keep answers within the boxes provided

My answer (in between 150 and 300 words)

My answer continued

Marker's comments: do not write in this box

Paper 40

The second coming of the Lord Jesus Christ (Part A)

Mark 13:1-23

Q1 **What discussion triggers the disciples' questions and Jesus' teaching about His second coming? (vv.1–3)**

- ☐ The temple's greatness and its stones
- ☐ Judaism
- ☐ Fear of Gentile nations

Q2 **Name five of the things which Jesus says are 'the beginnings of sorrows'. (vv.5–8)**

____

____

____

Q3 **What does God want all the persecution of verse 8 lead to? (vv.9–10)**

- ☐ Testimony to Jesus and preaching the gospel to all nations
- ☐ Fear and hiding
- ☐ Diluted Christianity

Q4 **Who will help persecuted Christians to say the right words in those trying times? (v.11)**

- ☐ A well-known male Christian leader
- ☐ Amnesty International
- ☐ The Holy Spirit

Q5 **What comfort is there in the face of cruel opposition even from one's own family? (vv.12–13)**

- ☐ All Christians who endure that cruelty will be saved
- ☐ No comfort
- ☐ Others are suffering too

Q6 **Whatever the 'abomination of desolation' may be, what will it cause people to do? (vv.14–18)**

- ☐ Flee away immediately
- ☐ Stay where they are and say nothing
- ☐ Hide in a cave

Q7 **How bad and intense will the suffering and opposition be in that time of tribulation? (v.19)**

- ☐ Not too bad
- ☐ As bad as in World War II
- ☐ Unprecedented since the creation of the world

Q8 **For whose sake will God shorten these days of horrific tribulation so that some will be saved? (v.20)**

- ☐ For the Romans
- ☐ For Christians—namely the elect whom He chose
- ☐ For Jewish leaders

Q9 **Against whom does Jesus warn in advance that they will falsely claim that Christ has come? (vv.21–23)**

- ☐ Jewish exorcists
- ☐ Temple worshippers
- ☐ False christs and false prophets

Marker's comments: do not write in this box

Paper 40 – Advanced Study

Students for the Advanced Study should answer one of A, B or C below

A. **What is the main thrust of Jesus' answer when the disciples ask Him for the timetable of His second coming?**
Mark 13:1–6; Mark 13:21–23

B. **Why should opposition and persecution increase our confidence that Christ will come again?**
Mark 13: 9–13; Luke 21:8–28

C. **With increasing tribulation, what comfort is it to know that Christ will return?**
Mark 13:19–23

PLEASE keep answers within the boxes provided

My answer (in between 150 and 300 words)

My answer continued

Marker's comments: do not write in this box

Paper 41

The second coming of the Lord Jesus Christ (Part B)

Mark 13:24-37

Q1 **Before Jesus comes in the clouds with great power and glory where will signs appear? (vv.24–26)**

- ☐ In the heavens
- ☐ In the sea
- ☐ In the mountains

Q2 **Then from where will His angels gather together Christians, namely the elect? (v.27)**

- ☐ From Jerusalem
- ☐ From the sea
- ☐ From as far and wide as you can get

Q3 **Just as the ripening of a fig tree heralds summer, so these signs will herald something. What? (vv.28–30)**

- ☐ The coming of Pentecost
- ☐ The second coming to earth of Jesus, the Son of Man
- ☐ World war

Q4 **Although even heaven and earth will pass away, what will not pass away? (v.31)**

- ☐ The sun
- ☐ The sea
- ☐ The words of Jesus

Q5 **Who alone knows the exact time when the Son of God and Son of Man, Jesus, will come again? (v.32)**

- ☐ God the Father
- ☐ The archangel Gabriel
- ☐ The apostle Paul

Q6 **Because we do not know when the Lord is returning what does Jesus say we must we do? (v.33)**

- ☐ Get a concordance and a calculator
- ☐ Guess when He will return
- ☐ Take heed, watch and pray

Q7 **What does the short parable in verses 34 to 37 warn us against doing when Christ returns?**

- ☐ Not watching but sleeping (spiritually) at Christ's return
- ☐ Panic
- ☐ Guessing His time of arrival

Marker's comments: do not write in this box

Paper 41 – Advanced Study

Students for the Advanced Study should answer one of A, B or C below

A. **Why can you be absolutely certain that Christ will come again?**
Mark 13:31; John 14:2–3; 2 Thessalonians 1:7–10

B. **As a fig tree's growth signals the coming summer, what will signal Christ's return?** Mark 13:24–30

C. **What is the main challenge to the Christian about Christ's second coming?**
Mark 13:32–37; 1 John 3:2–3; Matthew 25:1–13

PLEASE keep answers within the boxes provided

My answer (in between 150 and 300 words)

My answer continued

Marker's comments: do not write in this box

Paper 42

Remembering—in advance! Mark 14:1-11

Q1 **Why don't the chief priests and scribes arrest Jesus at Passover the Feast of Unleavened Bread? (vv.1–2)**

- ☐ There are not enough soldiers on duty
- ☐ They are on holiday
- ☐ They fear uproar from the people

Q2 **Who visits Simon the leper's house in Bethany with a valuable alabaster flask of oil (or ointment)? (v.3)**

- ☐ A Sadducee
- ☐ A woman (Mary—Martha's and Lazarus' sister according to John 11:2)
- ☐ A centurion

Q3 **After Mary breaks the flask and pours the oil over Jesus' head, why is this criticised as a waste? (vv.3–5)**

- ☐ It could have been sold for cash for the poor
- ☐ Jesus doesn't need it
- ☐ It is too extravagant to do that

Q4 **In defending her for doing a good work, how does Jesus compare Himself with the poor? (vv.6–7)**

- ☐ They don't use oil like that, but He does
- ☐ The poor always are there but He will leave
- ☐ He is poor too

Q5 **What highest commendation is given by Jesus to Mary? (v.8)**

☐ That the oil was expensive

☐ That Mary was loving

☐ That she has done what she could

Q6 **What has Mary just done in advance at Simon's house? (v.8)**

☐ Remembered Jesus' birthday

☐ Anointed His body for burial

☐ Entered there without invitation

Q7 **Where will her anointing of the body of Jesus, in advance of His death, be remembered? (v.9)**

☐ In Israel

☐ In Rome

☐ Wherever in the whole world the gospel is preached

Q8 **How does Judas, the self-seeking treasurer, react to Mary's love and Jesus' response to it? (vv.10–11)**

☐ For cash, he plans to betray Jesus to the chief priests

☐ He sulks

☐ He repents of his sinful attitude and thefts

Marker's comments: do not write in this box

Paper 42 – Advanced Study

Students for the Advanced Study should answer one of A, B or C below

A. **How do the Passover and the Feast of Unleavened Bread picture the salvation from sin that Jesus Christ will bring?**
Exodus 12:1–36; 1 Corinthians 5:7–8

B. **Why is the woman (Mary) such a wonderful example and a challenge to us about how we should give to the Lord?**
John 12:1–3; Mark 14:3–9; 2 Samuel 24:21–24; Mark 12:41–44; 2 Corinthians 8:9; Galatians 2:20

C. **Contrast Mary's attitude with that of Judas Iscariot. How are they each now remembered?**
Mark 14:8–11; Luke 22:47–48; Matthew 27:3–5

PLEASE keep answers within the boxes provided

My answer (in between 150 and 300 words)

My answer continued

Marker's comments: do not write in this box

Paper 43

Passover — Mark 14:12-31

Q1 When do the Jews kill the Passover lamb, to be fulfilled in Jesus as the Lamb of God? (v.12)

- ☐ The first day of the year
- ☐ The last day of the year
- ☐ The first day of the feast of Unleavened Bread

Q2 After His disciples ask where to prepare Passover, where does Jesus send two of them? (vv.12–16)

- ☐ A large upper room in a house in the city
- ☐ The synagogue
- ☐ The temple

Q3 Jesus says follow a man with a water jar and speak to the master of the house. Do they do so? (vv.13–14)

- ☐ No
- ☐ Only after complaining it is unlikely to happen like that
- ☐ Yes

Q4 Finding the large upper room in the city house, as Jesus said, what do the two disciples do? (vv.15–16)

- ☐ Have a rest
- ☐ Go back and tell Jesus it worked out well
- ☐ Prepare the Passover

Q5 **At Passover, Jesus predicts His betrayal by a disciple. What does each one ask sorrowfully? (vv.17–21)**

☐ 'Who is the betrayer?'

☐ 'Is it I?'

☐ 'Surely you have got that wrong, Lord?'

Q6 **Does Mark say Jesus' body is damaged as He says 'This is my body' and 'This is my blood'? (vv.22–25)**

☐ Yes

☐ No

☐ Unsure

Q7 **After a hymn, Jesus' warning, and resurrection prediction, who says he will not stumble? (vv.26–29)**

☐ Peter

☐ James

☐ John

Q8 **After Jesus predicts Peter's denial, from whom does the 'death before denial' promise come? (vv.30–31)**

☐ Just Peter

☐ Peter, James and John

☐ Peter, then all the disciples after him

Marker's comments: do not write in this box

Paper 43 – Advanced Study

Students for the Advanced Study should answer one of A, B or C below

A. **In how many ways do these verses show again that Jesus is in control?** Mark 14:13–16; Mark 14:13–30

B. **Contrast Peter's over-confidence with Jesus' knowing he would fail. How should humility and trusting God interact?** Mark 14:29–31; John 18:27; Luke 22:31–34; 1 Corinthians 10:12; 2 Corinthians 12:10

C. **Of what do the broken bread and the cup of wine remind us? How does this relate to the fact that Jesus will come again?** Mark 14:22–25; 1 Corinthians 11:24–25

PLEASE keep answers within the boxes provided

My answer (in between 150 and 300 words)

My answer continued

Marker's comments: do not write in this box

Paper 44

Gethsemane

Mark 14:32-52

Q1 **What does Jesus ask Peter, James and John as He leaves the other disciples in Gethsemane? (vv.32–34)**

- ☐ Mount guard for Him
- ☐ Check on the other disciples
- ☐ Stay there and watch (meaning pray)

Q2 **As Jesus faces deep sorrow in facing His coming crucifixion, what does He pray, if God wills? (vv.34–36)**

- ☐ To avoid His coming suffering and death for us
- ☐ Judgement on His enemies
- ☐ For an angel to save Him

Q3 **How many times does Jesus find the three disciples asleep, and tell them, 'Watch and pray'? (vv.37–40)**

- ☐ Once
- ☐ Twice
- ☐ Three times

Q4 **On finding them asleep the third time, what does Jesus do? (vv.41–42)**

- ☐ Leaves
- ☐ Waits for them to wake up
- ☐ Tells them His hour has come and goes to meet His betrayer

Q5 **Who leads the armed mob to take Jesus after betraying who He is by a greeting and kiss? (vv.43–47)**

- ☐ A Roman soldier
- ☐ Judas Iscariot
- ☐ Pilate

Q6 **After the high priest's servant has his ear cut off how does Jesus challenge the armed mob? (vv.48–49)**

- ☐ He asks why they are armed and why they did not take Him earlier?
- ☐ He insults them
- ☐ No challenge

Q7 **What does Jesus say must be fulfilled? (v.49)**

- ☐ Roman law
- ☐ Judas' promise to the religious people opposing Jesus
- ☐ The Scriptures

Q8 **What action do all His 'supporters' take regarding Jesus, including one who was naked? (vv.50–52)**

- ☐ Stand and fight the enemy
- ☐ Try to bribe the armed mob to leave
- ☐ Forsake Him and flee

Marker's comments: do not write in this box

Paper 44 – Advanced Study

Students for the Advanced Study should answer one of A, B or C below

A. **Why do you think that Jesus is exceedingly sorrowful, even to death? What kind of things do you think would be in His mind based on His words elsewhere in Mark's Gospel?**
Mark 14:34; Mark 10:32–34; Mark 14:41–42

B. **Why are the disciples sleeping instead of praying? What should be your attitude about spending quality time in prayer?**
Mark 14:37–42; 1 Thessalonians 5:17; Luke 18:1; Philippians 4:6; Isaiah 40:31

C. **Contrast the attitudes of Judas and Jesus. What part does the Bible play in the thinking of Jesus at this time?**
Mark 14:43–49; Psalm 119:1–7

PLEASE keep answers within the boxes provided

My answer (in between 150 and 300 words)

My answer continued

Marker's comments: do not write in this box

Paper 45

When the rooster crows — Mark 14:53-72

Q1 Who sit on the Sanhedrin, or Council, to give Jesus an unconstitutional and unjust trial? (vv.53–55)

- ☐ A democratically elected parliament
- ☐ Chief priests, elders and scribes
- ☐ Pilate's puppets

Q2 While Peter follows at a distance into the servants' courtyard, what does the Council try to do? (vv.55–59)

- ☐ Get Jesus condemned through perjury and fake accusations
- ☐ Seek justice
- ☐ Please Pilate

Q3 When the false witnesses can't agree and Jesus will not answer the high priest, what is He asked? (vv.55–61)

- ☐ 'Will you plead guilty?'
- ☐ 'Are you the Christ, the Son of the Blessed?'
- ☐ 'Are you not a perjurer?'

Q4 How does Jesus answer when asked who He really is? (vv.61–62)

- ☐ He confesses He is the Divine Christ and will come again in power
- ☐ Nothing
- ☐ He says He is a prophet

Q5 What now happens to the Lord Jesus Christ, the eternal Son of Man and Son of God? (vv.63–65)

- ☐ Nothing
- ☐ He escapes
- ☐ He is wrongly condemned to death for blasphemy, spat on, beaten and ridiculed

Q6 **How many times does Peter now deny that he knows Jesus? (vv.66–71)**

- ☐ Once
- ☐ Twice
- ☐ Three times

Q7 **What is worse about Peter's third denial, before the rooster crows the second time? (v.71)**

- ☐ He breaks down and cries
- ☐ He hits the person posing the question
- ☐ He begins to curse and swear as well

Q8 **What two things does Peter do after he hears the rooster crow twice and remembers Jesus' words? (v.72)**

- ☐ He thinks and weeps
- ☐ He swears again and storms off
- ☐ He gets drunk and blames others

Q9 **Why do you think it is important that people who say they love Christ stay close to Him each day?**

____

____

____

Marker's comments: do not write in this box

Paper 45 – Advanced Study

Students for the Advanced Study should answer one of A, B or C below

A. **What injustices against Jesus are there here? Did Jesus complain? Do you ever complain?**
Mark 14:55–65

B. **What causes Peter to fall in the way that he does at this time?**
Mark 14:54; Mark 14:66–71

C. **Why do you think Peter weeps? Contrast mere remorse with the Bible's teaching about real repentance and its effects.**
Mark 14:72; Hebrews 12:16–17; 2 Corinthians 7:10; 2 Peter 3:9

PLEASE keep answers within the boxes provided

My answer (in between 150 and 300 words)

My answer continued

Marker's comments: do not write in this box

Paper 46

Confession and silence — Mark 15:1-5

Q1 **Next morning, the religious leaders who want Jesus dead consult and take Him to Pilate. Why? (vv.1–2)**

- ☐ Pilate can execute Him if, as 'King of the Jews', He opposes Rome
- ☐ Frustration
- ☐ To annoy Pilate

Q2 **When Pilate asks Jesus if He is 'King of the Jews' does Jesus deny it, hesitate, or confess He is? (v.2)**

- ☐ Denies it
- ☐ Hesitates
- ☐ Confesses it

Q3 **When Jesus is accused falsely before Pilate by the chief priests, how does He answer? (v.3)**

- ☐ He deliberately answers nothing
- ☐ He defends Himself
- ☐ He does not know how to answer

Q4 **When Pilate raises the same questions (but not about who Jesus is), how does Jesus answer? (vv.4–5)**

- ☐ He deliberately answers nothing
- ☐ He defends Himself
- ☐ He does not know how to answer

Q5 **What does Pilate do as a result? (v.5)**

- ☐ He loses his temper
- ☐ He ridicules Jesus
- ☐ He marvels

Q6 **Who really seems in dignified control of the proceedings, despite being in the minority? (vv.1–5)**

- ☐ Pilate
- ☐ Jesus
- ☐ The ruling Jewish leaders

Q7 **What strengths and weaknesses are there in people found in this passage? How do you compare? (vv.1–5)**

Q8 **What about Jesus touches you most in this passage? (vv.1–5)**

Marker's comments: do not write in this box

Paper 46 – Advanced Study

Students for the Advanced Study should answer one of A, B or C below

A. **What do you learn about Pilate?**

Mark 15:1–5; Matthew 27:1–26; John 18:29—19:19; Luke 23:18–25

B. **What kinds of questions does Jesus answer immediately and why?** Mark 15:2–5

C. **When is silence justified? Illustrate from Jesus' behaviour. How should that work out in your daily life?**

Mark 15:3–5; James 1:19; James 3:2–13

PLEASE keep answers within the boxes provided

My answer (in between 150 and 300 words)

My answer continued

Marker's comments: do not write in this box

Paper 47

Anyone's son—Barabbas Mark 15:6-15

Q1 **Write a few sentences to explain who Barabbas is and why he can be released at Passover feast. (vv.6–7)**

Q2 **Is the custom of releasing a convicted criminal through popular opinion at Passover fair and just? (v.6)**

- ☐ Never
- ☐ Sometimes
- ☐ Always

Q3 **What do you think Pilate really wants to do with Jesus? Say from which verse(s) you get your view.**

Q4 **Why does Pilate think the chief priests hand over Jesus and stir up the crowd to have Him killed? (v.10)**

- ☐ Cruelty
- ☐ Envy
- ☐ To make it hard for Pilate

Q5 **As the cries of 'Crucify Him!' sound out, does Pilate get an answer to his question in verse 14? (vv.13–14)**

☐ Yes

☐ No

Q6 **Why finally does Pilate release Barabbas and have Jesus scourged and delivered to be crucified? (v.15)**

☐ He weakened because he wanted to please the crowd

☐ He liked Barabbas

☐ He did not respect Jesus

Q7 **Is there a danger of trying to please people rather than God?**

☐ Yes

☐ No

Marker's comments: do not write in this box

Paper 47 – Advanced Study

Students for the Advanced Study should answer one of A, B or C below

A. **Who is Barabbas? Why is he being set free?**
Mark 15:6–15; Luke 23:18–25

B. **Who orchestrates the vicious opposition against Jesus? Does being a religious leader mean that the person concerned automatically knows God in his life?**
Mark 15:9–11; John 3:1–21

C. **If after his release Barabbas did see Jesus dying between his two dying criminal friends, what thought would have struck him most? Do you see Jesus dying on the cross personally for you?** Romans 7:24; Luke 18:13; Romans 5:8; Galatians 2:20

PLEASE keep answers within the boxes provided

My answer (in between 150 and 300 words)

My answer continued

Marker's comments: do not write in this box

Paper 48

At the cross (Part A) — Mark 15:16-22

Q1 **Note down single words to describe the bullying and mockery which Jesus suffers. (vv.16–20)**

Q2 **In mocking Jesus, what title do they use for Him and who taught them that title? (Compare v.18 with v.9)**

- ☐ As a priest—from the chief priest
- ☐ As a criminal—from Barabbas
- ☐ As King of the Jews—from Pilate

Q3 **Isaiah 53 predicts Christ's crucifixion hundreds of years earlier. How does verse 7 explain these verses?**

Q4 **Who is made to carry the cross for Christ, and where is he from? (v.21)**

- ☐ Simon from Cyrene, North Africa
- ☐ Nicodemus from Jerusalem
- ☐ Lazarus from Bethany

Q5 **In all of this suffering and shame, how much is Jesus recorded as saying? (vv.16–22)**

- ☐ Many words
- ☐ A few complaints
- ☐ Nothing at all

Q6 **Wine mixed with myrrh dulls pain and therefore the senses. What does Jesus do when offered it? (v.23)**

- ☐ He gulps it down
- ☐ He refuses it
- ☐ He drinks a small amount of it

Marker's comments: do not write in this box

Paper 48 – Advanced Study

Students for the Advanced Study should answer one of A, B or C below

A. **Why does Jesus, the Son of Man, allow Himself to be bullied and beaten?** Mark 15:16–20; Psalm 86:14; Psalm 140:4

B. **When Jesus is mocked how does He react? How should you react if people mock you for being a Christian?**
Mark 15:19–20; Matthew 5:44; Isaiah 53:7

C. **Consider Mark 8:34 and Mark 15:21. What does it mean to take up the cross? What ordeal must Jesus face as He takes up His cross? What does Jesus do for you in dying on His cross?**
Mark 8:34; Mark 15:21; John 19:1; Luke 14:27;
1 Corinthians 15:31; Galatians 2:20; 1 Peter 2:24

PLEASE keep answers within the boxes provided

My answer (in between 150 and 300 words)

My answer continued

Marker's comments: do not write in this box

Paper 49

At the cross (Part B) Mark 15:23-32

Q1 **Does Jesus persuade the soldiers to help Him fulfil the prophecy of Psalm 22:18? (v.24)**

- ☐ No—he is dying on the cross
- ☐ Yes—auto suggestion to fulfil prophecy
- ☐ Yes—he whispers to them

Q2 **At the Jewish third hour (6.00 am) what is displayed above Jesus as He is crucified? (vv.25–26)**

- ☐ Blasphemer
- ☐ Rebel against Roman rule
- ☐ The King of the Jews

Q3 **What other Old Testament prophecy is fulfilled as Jesus is crucified between two robbers? (vv.27–28)**

- ☐ None
- ☐ Isaiah 53:12
- ☐ Isaiah 9:6

Q4 **What do the mocking blasphemers deliberately misquote and mislead the crowd about? (v.29)**

- ☐ Jesus predicting His resurrection in John 2:18–22
- ☐ Jesus saying Jerusalem will fall
- ☐ Jesus' prayers

Q5 **What do they challenge Him to do? (v.30)**

- ☐ Strike them dead
- ☐ Disappear
- ☐ Save Himself and come down from the cross

Q6 **Who joined in similar cruel mocking of Jesus and taunting challenges to Him? (vv.31–32)**

- ☐ Pharisees and Sadducees
- ☐ Chief priests, scribes and crucified criminals
- ☐ Roman soldiers

Q7 **If Jesus did not die on the cross bearing our sins and taking our punishment, could we ever be saved?**

- ☐ Yes: I am good
- ☐ Yes: I go to church
- ☐ No: 'there was no other good enough to pay the price of sin'

Marker's comments: do not write in this box

Paper 49 – Advanced Study

Students for the Advanced Study should answer one of A, B or C below

A. **Consider the phrase 'they crucified Him'. Who are 'they'? How do you react to the Creator God bleeding and dying to become your Saviour?** Mark 15:24–26; Mark 15:1, 3, 8, 9, 11, 13–14, 15, 16, 22–23; Philippians 2:5–11; Acts 20:28

B. **What do the fulfilled prophecies of Psalm 22:18 and Isaiah 53:12 teach you about the divine inspiration and factual accuracy of the Bible?** Psalm 22:18; Isaiah 53:12; Acts 13:23–30

C. **If Jesus had saved Himself by coming down from the cross, who else could He have saved from the punishment for their sins? By bearing our sins and judgement for those sins on the cross, who can He save now from eternal punishment?** Mark 15:29–32; Mark 10:45; 1 Timothy 2:6; 1 Peter 1:18–19; Isaiah 53:4–6; 1 Peter 2:24

PLEASE keep answers within the boxes provided

My answer (in between 150 and 300 words)

My answer continued

Marker's comments: do not write in this box

Paper 50

At the cross (Part C) Mark 15:33-39

Q1 What engulfs not only the cross where Jesus dies but also the whole land for three hours? (v.33)

- ☐ Rain
- ☐ Snow
- ☐ Darkness

Q2 What is the translated meaning of Jesus' cry from the cross, 'Eloi, Eloi, lama sabachthani?' (v.34)

- ☐ 'Elijah, Elijah, save me'
- ☐ 'My God, My God, why have you forsaken me?'
- ☐ 'Help me!'

Q3 Why is the incarnate God the Son forsaken by God the Father on the cross? (v.34)

- ☐ He bears our sins and God's judgement against them
- ☐ He fails
- ☐ God the Father doesn't love Him

Q4 Who and what do some wrongly think Jesus is calling for, probably because of the name 'Eloi'? (v.35)

- ☐ Rescue by Elijah
- ☐ Deliverance by God's great storm
- ☐ Intervention by the Elders of Jerusalem

Q5 **While some offer Him sour wine to drink in a sponge on a reed, what do others wonder? (vv.35–36)**

☐ Whether He will die

☐ Whether Elijah will come to take Him down

☐ Whether He will drink sour wine

Q6 **What does Jesus do before He breathes His last breath? (See Luke 23:46 before you answer.) (v.37)**

☐ Asks for another drink

☐ Criticises the chief priests and cruel soldiers

☐ Cries out with a loud voice

Q7 **After the temple veil is torn in two from top to bottom, what does the Centurion realise? (vv.38–39)**

☐ Jesus, although a man, is also 'the Son of God'

☐ His men mock Jesus

☐ The two criminals are dead

Q8 **Read Hebrews 9:1–5. What do you think the tearing of the veil from the top to the bottom means? (v.38)**

☐ The way to approach God is open now that Jesus has died on the cross

☐ Nothing

☐ Bad veil design

Marker's comments: do not write in this box

Paper 50 – Advanced Study

Students for the Advanced Study should answer one of A, B or C below

A. **As Christ bears our sin, darkness falls over the land. Jesus, God the Son, is forsaken for the first and only occasion in time or eternity by God the Father. Why?** Mark 15:33–34; 1 Peter 2:24; 1 Peter 3:18; Isaiah 53:4; Isaiah 53:10–11; John 14:6

B. **What mistake is made about Jesus' cry on the cross? What mistakes do people make about the cross today?** Mark 15:34–35

C. **Consider how the Roman centurion responds at the cross to the death of Jesus. How does he also respond in Luke 23:47? Why do his two responses blend so well together?** Mark 15:39; Luke 23:47; Romans 1:3–4; 1 Timothy 3:16; John 1:14

PLEASE keep answers within the boxes provided

My answer (in between 150 and 300 words)

My answer continued

Marker's comments: do not write in this box

Paper 51

He is risen! Mark 15:40–16:8

Q1 **Who among the women at Jerusalem, including those serving Jesus, observe the cross from afar? (v.40)**

- ☐ Mary Magdalene, Mary—James and Joses' mother, and Salome
- ☐ None
- ☐ Jesus' mother, Mary

Q2 **Councillor Joseph of Aramathea bravely asks Pilate for Jesus' body. What does Pilate first do? (vv.42–45)**

- ☐ He marvels that Jesus is already dead and verifies it with the Centurion
- ☐ Nothing
- ☐ He just says 'Yes'

Q3 **What does he then do? (v.45)**

- ☐ He says nothing to Joseph
- ☐ He promises the body later
- ☐ He grants Jesus' body to Joseph

Q4 **Joseph wraps the corpse, lays it in his tomb and seals it with a rock. Who sees where this is? (vv.46–47)**

- ☐ Mary Magdalene and Mary, mother of Joses
- ☐ Peter and John
- ☐ Salome and Nicodemus

Q5 **Are the women bringing anointing spices to the tomb after the Sabbath those found in Q1? (vv.1–2)**

- ☐ Yes
- ☐ No

Q6 **Why is their biggest concern not a concern to them any more? (vv.3–4)**

- ☐ They arrive early, not late
- ☐ The very large stone sealing the tomb is rolled away
- ☐ They find the tomb

Q7 **Underline what the young man in the tomb says as they seek Jesus and see where He was laid? (vv.6–7)**

He'll be back soon

He's risen

He's not here

He wasn't here

Keep it quiet

He'll be in Galilee

Q8 **How would you describe the attitude and actions of the three women as they hear the angel? (v.8)**

- ☐ Very confident
- ☐ Overjoyed
- ☐ Scared stiff, amazed, tongue-tied, and keen to get away?

Marker's comments: do not write in this box

Paper 51 – Advanced Study

Students for the Advanced Study should answer one of A, B or C below

A. **What facts here confirm the resurrection of the Lord Jesus Christ? Why is it important to demonstrate that Jesus really did rise from the dead?** Mark 15:42–47; Mark 16:3–7; Acts 1:3

B. **How do you know that the stone is rolled away from the tomb not to let Jesus out but to let people in? What biblical reasons can you give why Jesus' resurrection is absolutely vital?** Mark 16:3–6; 1 Corinthians 15:3–9; 1 Corinthians 15:12–19; Romans 1:1–4; Acts 2:32–36

C. **Why do the fear of the frightened women, the unbelief of doubting Thomas, and the hostility of persecutor Saul (who became the apostle Paul) help to confirm that Jesus rose from the dead? What do their fear, unbelief and hostility turn into?** Mark 16:8; Luke 24:9–11; John 10:24–29; Acts 26:1–23

PLEASE keep answers within the boxes provided

My answer (in between 150 and 300 words)

My answer continued

Marker's comments: do not write in this box

Paper 52

Resurrection, preaching, ascension — Mark 16:9-20

Q1 **How do the hearers react to news from Mary Magdalene and the two walkers that Jesus is risen? (vv.9–13)**

- ☐ With ecstatic joy
- ☐ With anger
- ☐ They do not believe the news

Q2 **When Jesus then appears to the eleven disciples what does He say to them about not believing? (v.14)**

- ☐ He rebukes their hard hearts
- ☐ He says they are right to be sceptical
- ☐ He says its all part of faith

Q3 **Where does Jesus tell them that they must go to preach the gospel urging people to be saved? (vv.15–16)**

- ☐ Just in church
- ☐ Just in their home towns
- ☐ In all the world

Q4 **To make it clear that their early gospel preaching has His authority, what will Jesus provide? (vv.17–18)**

- ☐ Lots of money
- ☐ Special specific signs for believers
- ☐ Sinless lives of ever perfect health

Q5 **After Jesus speaks to them and then is received into heaven (the ascension) what happens? (vv.19–20)**

- ☐ They preach everywhere and God provides their signs of authority
- ☐ They sleep
- ☐ We do not know

Marker's comments: do not write in this box

Paper 52 – Advanced Study

Students for the Advanced Study should answer one of A, B or C below

A. **See verses 13 and 14. Does everyone immediately believe in Jesus' resurrection? How does risen Jesus talk to some of them? What does that show about the resurrection and God's ability to change people?**
Mark 16:13–14; Luke 24:13–49; 1 Corinthians 15:3–9

B. **What are the main points of the gospel to be preached? Why should Christians share it with as many people as possible?**
Mark 16:15; 1 Corinthians 15:3–4; Luke 24:47; Matthew 28:18–20

C. **Could Jesus ascend into heaven, where He is seated now, without first rising from death? How is Jesus, as 'Emmanuel' ('God with us'), unlike any religious teacher, past or present?**
Mark 16:9; Mark 16:19; Acts 1:3; Acts 1:9–11; Hebrews 10:12; John 19:30; 1 Timothy 3:16; Ephesians 1:19–20; Philippians 2:9–11; Acts 4:12; John 14:6; Matthew 1:20–23

PLEASE keep answers within the boxes provided

My answer (in between 150 and 300 words)

My answer continued

Marker's comments: do not write in this box

Mark Time—the Study Course
A final word

Where do I go from here?

Christians do not read the Bible and pray every day to gain merit points! Neither are our daily 'Quiet Times' a kind of lucky charm to stop us having accidents or bad luck! Out of love for Christ we should discipline ourselves to spend quality time with Jesus every day, just as a loving husband and wife want to spend time together. Many folks with a 'normal' daily timetable get up earlier to make sure the day begins with God. Reading the Bible and praying are the best way to get to know Him better.

You may just have read through and studied a book of the Bible—Mark's Gospel—for the first time. Or you may have read and studied the Bible in depth before. But in any case, the important thing is to keep on reading the Bible seriously each day and to keep on praying. This daily privilege should be blended with treating each Sunday as the Lord's Day—the Christian Sabbath—and going regularly to worship and serve God in a church where people love Christ and His word. Don't flit about between churches. Find one, as near to you as possible, where you really feel at home and where you can be fed spiritually through good Bible ministry and warm, helpful fellowship both on the Lord's Day and at meetings during the week. Make sure you are loyal there and contribute to its life and service.

It might be wise now to recap on Mark by going through it all again, just to consolidate what you have just learned. You could profit greatly from that. Or you might now start to read through the New Testament, and then read through the Old Testament. Please see the Day One Publication book advertised inside the back cover called The Bible Panorama. That takes you through every book of the Bible and all its verses. Its Bible reading schemes in its Part 2 will help you through the Bible systematically and are simple to follow. It also answers some of tricky questions and objections that Bible-believing Christians often face. Whether you read the New or the Old Testament, or any book in either, it will be helpful, enjoyable and clear.

Most important of all, be sure that you are trusting Jesus Christ as your Lord and Saviour. He died upon that cruel cross to take your sins and the punishment for them that it would take you an eternity to pay. He rose again and lives today. He enters the lives and forgives the sins of all who receive Him, and gives eternal life now that continues in heaven after this life. That is how you come to know Christ. But if you know Him, you will want to get to know Him better every day. If you know Jesus Christ as your Saviour, may God bless you as you seek to know Him better every day!

Note to churches or organisations distributing this study book:

Please feel free to place a sticker over the CPR details below

Please submit completed booklet to:

CPR

CHRISTIAN PRISON RESOURCING

Christian **P**rison **R**esourcing
PO Box 61685
London
SE9 9BL